# Disc...

## Sutton...

*The story of five parishes*

**Douglas Cluett**

Sutton Heritage Service
1995

Published by Sutton Heritage Service
Central Library
St. Nicholas Way
Sutton
Surrey
SM1 1EA

ISBN: 0 907335 28 4

© London Borough of Sutton, 1995

All rights reserved. No part of the contents of this book may be reproduced or transmitted in any form or by any means without the written permission of the publisher.

# CONTENTS

| | |
|---|---|
| Introduction | 4 |
| In the Beginning | 5 |
| The Parishes from Domesday | 9 |
|   Beddington | 9 |
|   Carshalton | 16 |
|     St. Helier | 29 |
|   Cheam | 32 |
|     Worcester Park | 41 |
|   Sutton | 42 |
|     Belmont | 48 |
|   Wallington | 49 |
|     Beddington Corner | 52 |
|     Hackbridge | 54 |
|     Roundshaw | 56 |
| Historical Industries in the Borough | 57 |
| Further Information | 63 |
|   Books | 63 |
|   Buildings Open to the Public | 68 |

# INTRODUCTION

This book is a revised and enlarged version of a brief history of the Borough, written for, and published in, successive editions of the London Borough of Sutton's Official Guide. An earlier separate publication from the same source, but a direct offprint, was published as *Sutton Scene: a brief history of the London Borough of Sutton* in 1976. Many thanks to John Phillips, Heritage Manager, for his advice and help in the preparation and publication of this book; and to Shirley Edwards for designing it, as she has done for many of the publications I have been connected with in the past.

The five parishes are those old civil parishes, which, as the Boroughs of Sutton and Cheam and Beddington and Wallington, and the Urban District of Carshalton, merged in 1965 to form the London Borough of Sutton.

Doug Cluett, 1995.


## ILLUSTRATIONS ACKNOWLEDGEMENTS

All the pictures in this book can be found in the Archives and Local Studies Collection of Sutton Heritage Service, Central Library, Sutton. Photographs and illustrations are reproduced by kind permission of the following: Chorley & Handford, Courtauld Institute of Art.

# IN THE BEGINNING ...

## THE FIRST SETTLEMENTS

Even before the last Ice Age, about 10,000 years ago, the district was inhabited. The evidence for this is in the form of scattered finds of stone tools. As the ice retreated, Mesolithic hunters moved into the area, and, several thousand years later, around 4,000 BC, they were followed by the first farmers. Local evidence for this consists of a few finds from various locations and some traces of Early Bronze Age occupation in the grounds of Carshalton House.

We do not get any view of the overall landscape until the Late Bronze Age, around 900-700 BC. At this time there was a more or less circular enclosure on the site of what was, until very recently, Queen Mary's Hospital for Children, in Carshalton Beeches. At about the same time there was a hutted settlement on the later site of the Roman Villa, north of Carew Manor, Beddington. Work by the Museum of London in the 1980s has shown that there are traces of an extensive field system on the flat gravel lands between Beddington Park and Mitcham Common. Late Bronze Age material has also recently been found at Carshalton House, and on the site of the former Wandle Valley Hospital at Beddington Corner.

## THE ROMAN PERIOD

The Romans left many traces of themselves and their influence in the area; of which the most important are the remains of a villa at Beddington. This first came to light in 1871, when a bath house with a hypocaust (under-floor heating) was found whilst the Beddington Sewage Farm was being constructed. Recent excavations rediscovered the bath house and uncovered part of the villa and its outbuildings. It was this excavation which also disclosed the Late Bronze Age settlement mentioned above.

Two Roman, or Romano-British, coffined burials have been found at Beddington: one, a lead coffin, found in c.1873, is in Beddington Church; the other, a stone coffin containing a skeleton, together with some fragments of coloured glass, was found during the laying of a water main in Beddington Park in 1930. The length of the coffin, about seven feet (although the female skeleton within was 5 feet 9½ inches tall, according to the then Rector) was found in circumstances which gained the find considerable press publicity; even prompting an American magazine to publish a lavishly illustrated and imaginative account of the finding of the body of 'Queen Boadicea', 6 feet 7 inches tall, at Beddington, England. The coffin is now housed in the Dovecote in Beddington Park, and can be seen when the latter is open to the public.

In 1974, during the digging of a new grave in the northern part of Bandon Hill Cemetery, Beddington, a Romano-British cinerary urn containing the remains of a cremated body was found. Indications of similar burials, discovered later, suggest that this land was a burial ground some sixteen centuries or more ago, a strange re-use of the same piece of land for the same purpose after such an interval.

So many Roman remains were said to be present at Woodcote (at the southern end of Wallington) by the early antiquaries (Camden, Aubrey and others) that Woodcote was claimed by Camden to be the site of the 'lost' Roman town of Noviomagus, mentioned in Roman and later itineraries as being ten or fifteen miles from London on the road to Rochester and Canterbury.

Needless to say, other places around London have also been nominated for this distinction, and there may have been more than one Noviomagus. Chichester is now considered to have been so named (the name is usually translated as 'Newmarket'). The remains seen around Woodcote were probably those of the lost medieval village of that name.

The Roman road Stane Street, from London to Chichester, cuts across the east of the Borough, leaving a version of its name to Stonecot Hill; and a probable minor Roman road ran along Coldharbour Lane (now Purley Way) on the border with Croydon. Roman coins and objects have been found in many places in the Borough. The Roman legions left, and by the 6th century A.D., Anglo-Saxon invaders were displacing or absorbing the native Celts; and it is in this period that most of our local place names had their origins.

## THE SPRING-LINE VILLAGES

The origin of the historic villages which provided the focal points of modern settlement is unknown, but it is clear that water supply is the particular key to their location. Here, along the northern edge of the North Downs, there is a narrow belt of Thanet sand, from Croydon to Epsom, between the clay to the north and chalk to the south. Water descending through the deep chalk meets the relatively impermeable clay, and rises through the sand to give the abundant springs and ponds so long characteristic of the district, though now less prominent than they once were. Along this line of water there arose, from early times, settlements or villages strung out like beads on a necklace: eventually becoming, from east to west, Croydon, Waddon, Beddington, Wallington, Carshalton, Sutton, Cheam, Cuddington, Ewell and Epsom.

# PLACE NAMES

Seemingly the earliest time we find any of the place names written is in a charter in the Chertsey Abbey Cartulary, dated A.D. 727, but which by internal evidence could not be later, if genuine, than A.D. 674. From this we get Suthtone (Sutton), Æweltone (Carshalton), Cegeham (Cheam) and Bedintone (Beddington); names whose meanings are discussed later. The document in question records alleged gifts of lands in the above places, and elsewhere, by Frithwald, Subregulus (or under-king) of Surrey to Chertsey Abbey. This charter is generally considered to be a 13th century copy, or reconstruction, of an earlier document, or documents, passed off as original to establish claims to land ownership - a not uncommon medieval practice. Such documents, however, usually contain records of genuine transactions (although often mixed with some spurious material) and need not be ignored.

In Saxon times, Surrey, in common with many other English counties, or shires, was divided into 'hundreds' (a term of which the exact significance is in doubt). The local hundred was the Hundred of Wallington, or Waleton; and the Hundred Court, the instrument of financial and judicial local government (usually held in the open air) would have met in or near the settlement from which it drew its name, roughly in the centre of the Hundred. The Hundred of Wallington included not only the whole of the present London Borough of Sutton, but also the surrounding parishes of Addington, Chaldon, Coulsdon, Croydon, Mitcham, Morden, Sanderstead and Woodmansterne. This area contrasts with that of the Hamlet of Wallington - a hamlet being a small village, usually without a church of its own - the settlement itself being within the Parish of Beddington.

# THE PARISHES FROM DOMESDAY

In 1086, when the Norman Conquest was twenty years old, the great survey which became known as the Domesday Survey, of all lands in the Kingdom of England to assess their taxable value, was undertaken.

## BEDDINGTON

Beddington or Beddintone (thought to be derived from Beada's Tun; Beada's farm, or settlement) appears twice in the Domesday Survey, and there were evidently at least two manorial holdings under this name. One was held by Robert de Wateville as tenant of Robert de Tonbridge. The assets included two mills worth 40s (these would have been watermills on the Wandle - windmills are not known to have existed in England until over a hundred years later), 24 acres of meadow, a wood yielding five hogs, and fifteen houses in London.

The other manor was held by William FitzTurold from Miles Crispin. The identity of this manor is the subject of much discussion among local historians, and the picture is not clear. There is not space here to deal with this properly; nor, in detail, with questions of the locations then of the four settlements within the parish of Beddington for which there were tax returns in 1332: Bandon, Beddington, Wallington and Woodcote. Bandon and Woodcote are 'lost' villages, and Beddington, as well as Wallington (see below), may have 'moved'. Beddington may have been within the present-day Beddington Park, before being combined with Bandon on its present site; the name of Bandon then giving way to the name of the Parish.

1. The Plough, Beddington, c.1912. There has been an inn on this site since at least the early 18th century; this present one was built around 1900.

The Wateville family kept the first manor (or Home-Beddington) until 1159, and at some point between then and 1196 it passed into the hands of the crown in unknown circumstances. It was regranted to a succession of people, and was later held for a rent of a wooden crossbow worth 12d a year, every Whitsuntide. It was subsequently given to Richard and Elizabeth Wylughby, who, in 1352, were granted licence to lease it for life to Nicholas Carew, who later married their daughter Lucy, widow of Thomas Huscarl, heiress to the Beddington manor of Huscarls (probably the second Domesday manor).

# The Carews

Thus the Carew family entered on the local scene as landowners. A cadet branch of a well-known family of part Norman origin, by the 12th century established at Carew in Pembrokeshire, from which they took their name, the Beddington Carews became important and famous in their own right, and came to own much land in Surrey and Sussex. Their name was to be borne locally for another five hundred years.

The manor house of the Carews, now Carew Manor School, still stands by the ancient church of St. Mary the Virgin, on the edge of Beddington Park (a name by which the house itself was known in the past). Its oldest part above ground is the Great Hall, with its hammer-beam and arch-braced roof (probably late 15th century). It is now known that the Manor House was moated during the 16th and 17th centuries, and probably earlier.

Perhaps the most famous of the Beddington Carews was Sir Nicholas Carew, K.G. He was the son of Sir Richard Carew, Sheriff of Surrey. He himself was Sheriff of Surrey and Sussex in 1518-19 and was a courtier and favourite of Henry VIII, to whom he was Master of the Horse. In 1539, however, he was accused of high treason, and beheaded, for his alleged part in the Pole Plot to dethrone Henry. A family tradition was said to exist that the real reason for his downfall arose from a quarrel with the King over a game of bowls, in the course of which insults were delivered which Henry could not forgive. However, court faction intrigue, together probably with Henry's wish for more land in this area to add to his hunting palace of Nonsuch, then being built, are the basic causes of his dispatch.

Beddington Manor, with other Carew lands, was forfeited to the King, and the house used as an extra Royal residence; a park being enclosed for hunting. Henry had made a recorded visit to Sir Nicholas there in 1531, probably with Anne Boleyn.

The house and manor were later restored by Mary I to Nicholas's son, Sir Francis Carew. Sir Francis was a celebrated Elizabethan horticulturist. Queen Elizabeth I visited him at least fifteen times at Beddington, and there is a story of his delaying the ripening of a cherry tree by covering it with a canvas kept moist, so that the fruit should be at its best for one of her visits. She is also said to have particularly liked the wooded walk, part of which still remains, known as Queen Elizabeth's Walk.

Sir Francis's sister Anne was married to Sir Nicholas Throckmorton, ambassador to France. Francis never married, and he named as his heir Anne's son Nicholas, whose sister Elizabeth (Bess) married Sir Walter Ralegh.

Francis created one of the most remarkable Elizabethan gardens, full of grottoes, water features, and other conceits, and is traditionally credited with trying out at Beddington various exotic plants brought back by Ralegh from the New World, possibly including tomatoes, potatoes and tobacco. This may or may not be so; but the popular belief that Sir Francis's famous orangery came from the same source is unfounded, since the orange tree is not a native New World plant, and arrived there via Europe from Asia.

Whilst Sir Francis did not grow the very first orange trees in England, he was almost certainly the first to grow them in quantity (he was in Paris in 1562 buying trees - oranges, lemons, myrtles and pomegranates), and his orangery was famous and unusual. The trees were planted in the open ground and protected in winter by a removable wooden shelter, or shelters, within which stoves were lighted. The present structure known as the Orangery Wall dates from the early 18th century, and was created by Sir Nicholas Carew (d. 1727), first Baronet, as part of a four-sided orangery built around Sir Francis's trees. Nevertheless, the trees perished, according to one writer, in the great frost of 1739-40, when the Thames froze over.

In 1611, the younger Nicholas Throckmorton changed his name to Carew on inheriting from his uncle, Sir Francis. When Ralegh was executed in 1618, his widow sent a hurried letter to her brother at Beddington requesting permission for her husband's body to be interred in the church there, and saying that it would be brought that night by two of her men. It is arguable that this was done, in spite of an entry in the register of St. Margaret's Westminster, but no investigation is possible at present since the Carew vault below the Carew chapel, in Beddington Parish Church, was sealed up in the late-19th century.

The later Carew, already mentioned, Sir Nicholas Carew the first Baronet, was important in the history of the house and gardens at Beddington. He took over his inheritance when he came of age in 1707, after a long period of guardianship, and did much rebuilding of the house and restructuring of the garden and its watercourses. As well as the Orangery Wall, the Dovecote, a remarkable building dedicated to breeding pigeons for food on a considerable scale (with nearly 1300 nesting boxes), belongs to this period.

His death in 1727 marks the end of the great days of the Carews, with the family fortunes now in a decline. A major factor may have been Carew's speculation in the South Sea Company, the sub-governor of which was his neighbour, Sir John Fellowes of Carshalton House. There was a second baronet; and then the latter's daughter, who died unmarried at the age of 27, ending the direct line of the Carews of Beddington in 1769.

2. The building now known as Carew Manor, Beddington, in 1828. This view shows the west front of the house created for Sir Nicholas Carew, 1st Baronet; with the parish church of St Mary's on the right.

The last three 'Carews' to hold Beddington were Carews in name only: Canadian-born Admiral Sir Benjamin Hallowell, later Carew; his son, Captain Charles Hallowell Carew; and his grandson, Charles Hallowell Hallowell Carew. The Admiral inherited from a cousin, Mrs. Anne Paston Gee, who had herself inherited from her husband's brother, a Carew descendant. In spite of her own tenuous connection, Mrs. Gee made it a condition of her will that Sir Benjamin should assume the Carew name and arms.

His grandson, Charles Hallowell Hallowell Carew, dissipated the remains of the family fortune by unsuccessful gambling, and in 1859 the estates had to be sold to pay his debts. The house was bought by the Lambeth Female Orphan Asylum (later the Royal Female Orphanage Asylum), and was thus occupied until the outbreak of the Second World War. It was extensively altered between 1859 and 1866. Before the First World War, the orphanage sold the first Baronet's wrought-iron gates and screen (the present ones in front of the house are facsimiles). They went to America, and are now in California, in the Huntington (which comprises a library, art collection, museum and botanical gardens), at San Marino, near Los Angeles.

The present Beddington Church, not the first, dates in part from the 13th century, and contains interesting tombs and memorial brasses, notably those relating to the Carews, as well as a fine Norman font.

# CARSHALTON

In 1086 the name appears as Aultone; later, Kersaulton and Cresaulton. The original 'Aulton' or 'Æwiell-tun' part of the name is taken to mean 'farm by the spring' The later 'Kers' or 'Cres' addition is probably linked with either cross (a cross-roads, perhaps with a cross erected) or cress - watercress (the district was once famous for cress, trout and walnuts).

The manorial history is complex. According to Domesday it had been held in the time of Edward the Confessor as five manors. In 1086 there was only one, held by Goisfrid, or Geoffrey, de Mandeville, who allotted a portion of it to his daughter when she married Geoffrey, son of the Count of Boulogne. The overlordship descended through the de Mandevilles, Earls of Essex, and the de Bohuns, Earls of Hereford and Essex, reverting to the crown in 1399 after the de Bohun heiress, Eleanor, married Thomas of Woodstock, a son of Edward III; and their son, Humphrey, died childless.

The name of the Boulognes or Bolonias, as tenants of the Manor, is probably the name which is really commemorated by the old well by Carshalton Church, now dry, traditionally known as Anne Boleyn's Well, which is linked with that unfortunate queen through a curious legend. The story was that the well originated from a stone kicked by her horse, causing a spring to gush forth, whilst she was riding through Carshalton on her way from Nonsuch Palace to Beddington Park. However, Anne was beheaded in 1536 and the building of Nonsuch was not begun until 1538. This does not, of course, prove that Anne could not have been riding through Carshalton on some other occasion; but the well was almost certainly of greater antiquity than the period of that lady's short life, and there was a chapel to 'Our Lady of Boulogne' nearby.

3. Carshalton Parish Church and 'Anne Boleyn's Well' (probably originally the medieval well of 'Our Lady of Boulogne').

After the Bolonias came the De Fiennes, with whom they were connected by marriage, and then a variety of tenants during the late 13th and 14th centuries, until, in the 1370s, the Carews added part of Carshalton to their holdings.

An interesting character who held the sub-manor of Stone Court from before 1448 until 1498 was Nicholas Gaynesford, or Gainsford, a member of a Crowhurst family with extensive land holdings in Surrey. Nicholas attended Parliament as a 'knight of the shire', and was several times Sheriff of Surrey. His period was that of the Wars of the Roses, and he lived through two Yorkist reigns and died in the reign of the Lancastrian Tudor Henry VII, who ended the Wars by victory at the Battle of Bosworth in 1485. Gainsford somehow managed to survive the power changes during the Wars of the Roses, although twice accused of being a traitor, once by Edward IV and once by Richard III; and on each occasion having his manor confiscated, only to regain it both times. His descendants held Stone Court until 1547, when his great-great-grandson, Robert, disposed of most of it, but Stone Court was still sometimes called Gainsford's Place until the early nineteenth century.

In or before 1549, Carshalton Manor passed to the St. Johns, allied by marriage to the Carews. Nicholas St. John sold a 'moiety' (or portion, originally a half) in 1580 to one Richard Burton, the other portion being conveyed, in 1590, to Walter Cole. The second moiety, after passing through the hands of Anne, Countess of Arundel, and her grandson Henry, Earl of Arundel, was purchased in 1696 by Sir William Scawen, who subsequently bought the other moiety, thus reuniting the Manor of Carshalton. Scawen was a merchant who had increased his fortune by backing William of Orange before his future as King William III of England was settled. He became in 1697,

Governor of the Bank of England, and a director of the East India Company, in 1710. His nephew and heir, Thomas, who inherited in 1722, proposed, following his uncle's wishes, to build a great new house in Carshalton Park to replace the then existing Manor House, a medieval building known as 'Mascalls'. The design, by Giacomo Leoni, was published in 1742 in Leoni's translation of *The Architecture of L.B. Alberti*; and a new Park Wall, two miles in length, was built, in which great gates of hammered iron were set. Some of this wall still stands.

The new house was never finished; and, early this century, the gates were sold, and went, at a remove, to the Long Island estate of an American millionaire. They still stand there, marking the entrance to what has become the New York State University's Agricultural and Technical Institute, a fate similar to that of the Beddington Park gates (the same agent, John Starkie Gardner, expert and prolific writer on wrought iron, was responsible for both sales).

In 1781, Carshalton Park and Manor were sold to George Taylor, who had made his money in the West Indies as a sugar planter, and who died in 1834. The Taylors held possession throughout the 19th century. Tenants at the turn of the century were the Colman family, of Colman's mustard fame. The house, known as Carshalton Park House, or Carshalton Place (which stood outside the area of the present park, near the High Street, at the junction of Brookside and Carshalton Place [road]), was pulled down in about 1927. It had probably been built after the abandonment of the Leoni House.

Carshalton Church, dedicated to All Saints, apparently dates in part from the 12th century. It was enlarged in the 13th century, with major alterations and additions made in the 18th, 19th, and

20th centuries. It includes monuments to Sir John Fellowes; Nicholas Gainsford, Sir William Scawen and many others of interest.

## Carshalton House

A major house of historical interest, which is still standing, is Carshalton House, now St. Philomena's Catholic School for Girls, at the west end of the old village. This was built, probably before 1707, by Edward Carleton, scion of an already well-established Carshalton family, on the site of an older house, which it incorporates. In 1713 he went bankrupt; and the house, on being sold two years later, was described as 'new built by the said Edward Carleton'. After Carleton it was briefly the home of Doctor John Radcliffe, founder of the Radcliffe Library and Observatory at Oxford, and physician to King William III and Queen Anne.

In spite of his distinguished practice he seems rather to have lacked a tactful bedside manner, since his bluntness about their disorders is said to have offended many of his patients, including King William.

He refused to attend Queen Anne in her last illness in 1714, because he was himself suffering from gout. He thereby incurred the hatred of the Tory and Jacobite parties, to whom her continued existence was important. It is only fair to say that his own illness was not trivial, since he died a few months later; his end, it is said, hastened by the threatening letters he received.

The house was briefly in the hands of Sir William Scawen as trustee, and then, in 1716, purchased by Sir John Fellowes, a director of the South Sea Company, who in 1718, became its

4. Cadets of the Ordnance School at Carshalton House, c.1850. Between 1848-59 the house was used as a school for the first time, for the education of Royal Artillery and Engineers Cadets. Lithograph by C.B. Moore.

Sub-Governor (or chief, as the King, George I, was theoretically Governor), and in 1719 given a Baronetcy. The house was
technically confiscated after the financial catastrophe known as the Bursting of the South Sea Bubble, in 1720, although Fellowes continued to live there until his death, together with his brother, who assumed ownership, and who lived there after Sir John.

Later owners or occupiers included Philip Yorke, who became Lord Chancellor and Earl of Hardwicke; Admiral Lord Anson, circumnavigator of the world (his son-in-law); and Thomas Walpole, nephew of Robert Walpole, Prime Minister, and cousin of Horace Walpole, famous diarist.

It afterwards became a military academy, and then 'a school for young gentlemen' before it was acquired in 1893 for its present purpose by the Daughters of the Cross. Carshalton House, together with its grounds and unique water pavilion and tower, are open to the public on certain days of the year - normally Easter and August Bank Holiday Mondays. Additionally the Water Tower, is opened to the public on a regular basis by the Friends of the Water Tower Trust during the summer months.

**Heritage Centre, Honeywood**

In December 1990, a Heritage Centre for the Borough was opened in an historic house known as Honeywood, which stands in a picturesque setting on the western edge of the Carshalton town ponds.

The core of Honeywood is a building of flint and clunch (hard chalk) which probably dates from the mid-seventeenth century. External walls of this building, with their decorative flint and

5. A view across Carshalton Ponds c.1911. Honeywood, now the Borough's Heritage Centre, is on the right.

chalk chequerwork, and, in one case, with a still-glazed window, were exposed during restoration, and remain on view. When the springs are flowing, a stream runs under the house and enters the Upper Pond. This may be a surviving feature from an earlier use of the building, perhaps an industrial one, as yet undetermined. There are early 19th century additions and updatings to the house, as well as late-Victorian and Edwardian wings.

Among former residents of the house was William Hale White ('Mark Rutherford'), a writer and philosopher connected to the Pre-Raphaelite and Arts and Crafts movements, both of which have a number of associations with the district. One of Hale White's sons married a daughter of Arthur Hughes, Pre-Raphaelite painter, who lived nearby at 'Wandle Bank' in Wallington.

The Heritage Centre displays permanent and temporary exhibitions on local history and related topics. It includes an Early Settlement Room, featuring in particular the Roman villa excavated at Beddington, and a Tudor Gallery telling the story of the area's major involvement in national affairs at this time, with emphasis on Henry VIII's Palace of Nonsuch, and his interplay and ultimate conflict with his once-favourite courtier Sir Nicholas Carew, K.G., of Beddington. There is a Wandle Room and a Commercial Room, a Childhood Room with a collection of toys treasured by a local resident from an Edwardian childhood; and a restored Edwardian Billiards Room. The latter includes an audio-visual presentation of the history of Honeywood's immediate surroundings. The Heritage Centre is in the care of Sutton Heritage Service, and is run with the help of a volunteer support organisation, The Friends of the Heritage Centre.

6. Dining room in Little Holland House, Carshalton. Almost everything visible was made by Frank Dickinson, who built the house.

## Little Holland House, Carshalton Beeches

Among those interested in Carshalton in the last century was the author John Ruskin; and in 1889, in the preface to his book *The Crown of Wild Olive*, he wrote, in what developed into a diatribe against the pollution of the River Wandle: "Twenty years ago there was no lovelier piece of lowland scenery in South England ... than that immediately bordering on the sources of the Wandle, and including the low moors of Addington and the villages of Beddington and Carshalton..."

One of the followers of the social and artistic ideals of John Ruskin and William Morris was a remarkable man named Frank Dickinson. He was a believer in self sufficiency; the dignity of labour; the beauties of nature; and the supremacy of the work of the hand over the work of the machine. Born into poverty in Paddington, in 1874, and leaving school at the age of thirteen, he developed great skill at a wide range of arts and crafts.

Becoming engaged to be married, he determined to build a house of which Morris and Ruskin would approve, and began to make furniture for it in the disused coal-cellar of his parents' home (which by now was in Streatham).

An interest-free loan from a Mutual Building Society enabled him, in 1902, to buy a plot of land and begin to build his 'ideal home' to his own design, with the aid of one of his brothers, and, initially, a bricklayer and labourer. Ruskin's words had drawn him to Carshalton, and his house was to be a country cottage in the then mainly undeveloped Carshalton Beeches area.

Frank and his bride moved into the still uncompleted house (now 40 Beeches Avenue) in 1904, and for almost the rest of his life Frank worked on, in, and around the house: carving beams and panelling; making fireplaces with carved, moulded and beaten-metal decorations; filling the house with a wealth of beautiful handmade objects: furniture, metalwork (including silverware) and paintings. In later years, he turned to writing. His autobiography (written in the last years of his life) and a volume of poems survive, as yet unpublished.

He died in 1961, leaving his house a testament to the Arts and Crafts movement, to his life and philosophy, and to his wife, who was the inspiration for it.

In 1972, the London Borough of Sutton had the opportunity to purchase the house and decided to restore it, maintain it, and open it, at specified times, to the public. Called Little Holland House after the house in Kensington in which the painter G.F. Watts (whom Dickinson also greatly admired) lived, the house was opened to the public in 1974, Frank Dickinson's centenary year. Two thousand people visited it within two weeks of its opening. It is now in the care of Sutton Heritage Service.

## The Oaks and The Derby

Another 'Great House' was The Oaks, on the edge of the North Downs, above Carshalton, once occupied by the Earls of Derby. This was formerly in the Parish of Woodmansterne, but was added to Carshalton after Urban District boundary changes in 1933.

It was named after a clump of trees known as 'Lambert's Oaks', which stood nearby; and was itself originally called by the fuller name. A house, or a succession of houses on the site, appears to have been the seat of the Lamberts of Banstead from at least the late 13th century to about 1660, when the family moved to another house, called Shortes Place, in Woodmansterne, and leased Lambert's Oaks to a succession of tenants.

By this time, horse racing and other sporting activities were well established on the downlands. Many of the house's lessees were attracted to it by this aspect of the Downs, and the first tenants appear to have been a group of 18th century gentlemen known as the Hunters' Club. It is not known how much building or rebuilding they may have done to the house, before, in about 1756, it was leased to General John Burgoyne; but subsequent rebuildings and additions involved at least two famous architects: Sir Robert Taylor and Robert Adam.

Burgoyne was the son-in-law of the 11th Earl of Derby, and known to history as the general who surrendered to the American forces at Saratoga in their War of Independence. He is also known for organising England's first 'Fête Champêtre', a rural outdoor feast or festival, at The Oaks, in 1774, to celebrate the betrothal of the Derby heir, Lord Stanley. He wrote a Masque, performed on this occasion, called *The Maid of the*

7. Interior view of the supper room and part of the ballroom in the temporary pavilion designed by Robert Adam for the Fête Champêtre at The Oaks, to celebrate the betrothal of the Earl of Derby's heir, in June 1774.

*Oaks*, later produced at Drury Lane. A Supper Pavilion designed by Robert Adam was built especially for the occasion. The Earl of Derby later took over the lease from Burgoyne.

Lord Stanley became 12th Earl of Derby in 1776. In 1779, whilst he was at dinner with the Duke of Richmond and Sir Charles Bunbury, a new horse race was instituted and named 'The Oaks', after the house. In the following year, in similar circumstances, another race was conceived. The story is that Lord Derby tossed a coin with Sir Charles Bunbury to see after whom the race should be named. Derby won; otherwise thousands would now flock to Epsom every year to see the Bunbury!

Sadly The Oaks was demolished in the late 1950s as the result of damage and dilapidation accruing from the Second World War.

## St. Helier

This 'London overspill' estate, for the rehousing of people from decaying inner London areas, was built between 1928 and 1936; the main building work being apparently done between early 1929 and the end of 1934. It was built by C.J. Wills and Sons for the London County Council, who had acquired for the purpose 825 acres which had been farmland, both arable and pasture. Much of this land had, in fact, been used for the local lavender and herb industry, to which the estate was more or less a final death blow.

The area chosen in 1926, south of Mitcham and west of the River Wandle, was then part of the Urban Districts of Merton and Morden; Carshalton; and Sutton and Cheam. It was the largest of the L.C.C. estates south of the Thames, and the second largest overall. The estate was designed as a 'garden city',

8. A post-war aerial view of St. Helier, looking eastwards. The large white building is St. Helier Hospital, opened in 1938, which stands in Wrythe Lane near the top of Rose Hill.

following the ideas of Sir Ebenezer Howard, founder of Letchworth and Welwyn garden cities: preserving as many as possible of the existing trees and natural features, and including many open spaces and sports and recreation grounds. It was hoped that greens, gardens, and shrubberies, backed by houses with bays and gables, would make the roads visually interesting and diverse. To this end 120 acres, more than an eighth of the site, were kept as open spaces. During building, much of the material was distributed about the estate by a specially-built light railway, communicating with sidings at Mitcham.

The area was intended to function as a community, or a series of communities, and for this purpose eighteen schools, seven churches, two large pubs, and the 2,000-seater Gaumont cinema (now a bingo hall) were built. Shops were constructed too, of course; sixty by 1938. There were 9,000 houses and flats, to accommodate 40,000 people. The huge St. Helier Hospital, a landmark for miles around, built near the top of Rose Hill, was opened in 1938. Here, in 1943, John Major, later to be Prime Minister, was born. His family lived in Worcester Park.

The roads, other than the major through roads, were named after monastic establishments in England and Wales. This was to commemorate the fact that Merton once had a notable priory; Morden once belonged to Westminster Abbey; Sutton to Chertsey Abbey; and Cheam to the Archbishop of Canterbury and the monastery of Christchurch, Canterbury. To help in locating roads, all were arranged alphabetically, with the A's in the north-west corner, ranging through the estate to the W's in the south-west.

The estate itself was named after Lady St. Helier, a former Alderman of the L.C.C. from 1910 to 1927 who had fought hard for the improvement of housing facilities in London, but who died in 1931 before the estate was completed. (St. Helier, Jersey, objected that the name would cause confusion, and suggested Jeuneville instead - Lady St. Helier was formerly Lady Mary Jeune.)

## CHEAM

In 1086 the name, from being Cegeham, appears as Ceiham. A suggested origin is Kaga- or Kagi-Hamm: village by the stumps, or underwood, or in a clearing. The Domesday Book says: 'The...Archbishop [Lanfranc] holds Ceiham for the sustenance of the Monks...'.

Lanfranc, close ally of William the Conqueror, was Archbishop of Canterbury from 1070 to 1089. Cheam had been given, in 1018, by Athelstan (also known as Lifing), Archbishop of Canterbury 1013-1020, to the monastery of Christchurch, Canterbury. Lanfranc, perhaps feeling that half of Cheam was quite enough for the sustenance of the monks, divided the manor in two, keeping East Cheam for himself and allotting West Cheam to them.

In 1540, with the dissolution of the monasteries, West Cheam was surrendered to the Crown and annexed to the Honour of Hampton Court. (An Honour was a group of manors administered together.) This was the time when Henry VIII, building Nonsuch Palace nearby, was collecting land in the district. In 1563, Elizabeth I sold West Cheam to the Earl of Arundel for £885 (Arundel at this time owned Nonsuch). It passed, as did Nonsuch, to his son-in-law, John, Lord Lumley, on Arundel's death in 1579. When Lumley died in 1609, West Cheam went to his nephew, Splandion Lloyd. In 1729 Roland

9. The Lumley Chapel in Cheam Churchyard, once the chancel of the medieval church.

Lumley Lloyd willed it to the Duke of Bedford, who sold it to Edward Northey (son of the Attorney General) in 1755, in the hands of whose family it remained for some time.

West Cheam Manor House was on the site where Cheam Library now stands. Little is known of its appearance except that it was built of brick. It was pulled down soon after 1796, at which time it was said to be in a poor state of repair.

East Cheam Manor was sold by Thomas Cranmer, when Archbishop of Canterbury, to Henry VIII in 1538, and this was also annexed to the Honour of Hampton Court. In 1554, however, Mary granted it to the newly-created Viscount Montagu, ennobled on the occasion of her marriage to Philip of Spain. In 1575 he sold it to Arundel, thus reuniting it with West Cheam.

In Cranmer's time the manor was leased to a man called Yerde from whom the tenancy passed to Thomas Fromond, his son-in-law, who built the manor house of East Cheam, which stood on the west side of Gander Green Lane, just north of Cheam Road. This was reputed to be a fine example of Tudor domestic architecture, but a surviving watercolour of it by Gideon Yates c.1810 shows a building of mixed periods, probably partly pre-Tudor. It was apparently pulled down around 1800 by Philip Antrobus, who built Lower Cheam House on its site. This in its turn was demolished in 1933.

Cheam is still rich in old buildings, including The Old Cottage in The Broadway, which dates from about 1480-1500, and which was moved a short distance to its present site in 1922 to make way for road widening. This, among its many former uses, was at one time the offices of Cheam Parish Council, and is probably the surviving wing of a medieval hall house.

The present parish church of Cheam, dedicated to St. Dunstan, was built in 1864, slightly north of the former church; of which the east end of the chancel, rich in memorials, some of which were moved from elsewhere in the church, was sealed off and preserved as a separate building, known as the Lumley Chapel.

The monuments there to the Lumley family are, of course, of special interest, with their Nonsuch connections; but there are many others, including a brass to Bartholomew, son and heir of Thomas Fromond, the builder of East Cheam Manor House. The earliest brass dates from 1450 (to John and Joan Compton). The old church itself, of which this fragment remains, was built by about 1230.

It is worthy of note that five out of six successive rectors of Cheam appointed between 1581 and 1624 became bishops; and one of them, George Mountain, Rector 1609-1617, went on to become Archbishop of York.

Two buildings in particular, both now demolished, linked Cheam with national history and brought the great and famous to the neighbourhood. These were Nonsuch Palace and Cheam School.

## Nonsuch Palace

The Palace lay between Cheam and Ewell. Its site is outside the Borough of Sutton but is in Nonsuch Park, owned and administered jointly by the London Borough of Sutton and the Borough of Epsom and Ewell. Nonsuch Park itself was part of Nonsuch Little Park, surrounding the Palace. Nonsuch Great Park extended across Ewell, Stoneleigh and Worcester Park, almost as far as Old Malden Station.

10. Nonsuch Palace, engraved by Joris Hoefnagel from his sketch made in 1568. Queen Elizabeth's coach is approaching from the south.

Nonsuch Palace was the conception of Henry VIII, who wanted a new palace to outshine the Renaissance palaces of his great rival, François I of France. From the first he called it 'None-such' because it was to be without peer or parallel.

Henry chose his site, convenient for a hunting palace within a day's ride of London and Hampton Court; acquired the manor, village, and church of Cuddington, which happened to be occupying it at the time, and began building in 1538. Cartloads of stone from the newly-demolished Merton Priory were incorporated in the foundations.

The main feature of the palace was the vast decorative (and symbolic) scheme for the southern half of the palace, with its high towers which included the royal apartments. This scheme utilised panels of stucco duro (hard plaster) mouldings and carvings, in high relief, separated by carved and gilded slate.

The basic structure of the palace was probably completed by 1540, but the decorative work was a long job, and some of it probably remained to be finished when Henry died in 1547. The palace left royal ownership when Mary I exchanged it, for four manors and a cash payment of £485 13s 4d, with Henry Fitzalan, 12th Earl of Arundel. Elizabeth I received it back from Arundel's son-in-law, Lord Lumley, who inherited it from Arundel, in payment of a debt. She was much attracted to Nonsuch, and used it frequently. It then remained a royal palace until 1649, when it was confiscated in the year of Charles I's execution. It was later restored to his widowed Queen. Twice, in 1665 and 1666, the Exchequer was moved to Nonsuch from London, at the times of the Plague and the Fire of London respectively.

The end of Nonsuch came when Charles II gave it to Barbara Villiers, Countess of Castlemaine, who sold it for the cost of its building materials, in 1682. It was demolished, and even its exact site was almost lost for many years, until its excavation in 1959. The foundations, unfortunately, had to be filled in again, to prevent deterioration of the chalk and sandstone materials that would otherwise have occurred; but three granite stones, one inscribed with a ground plan, now mark the site, straddling the main path through the park from Cheam to Ewell.

Displays of Nonsuch material can be seen locally in the Heritage Centre's Tudor Gallery and in Whitehall, Cheam; as well as in Bourne Hall Museum, Ewell, and in the British Museum and the Museum of London.

**Cheam School**

Cheam School existed in Cheam for some three hundred years. The exact date and circumstances of the founding of the school are still in doubt; but it now seems clear that it was in existence

11. Cheam School, c.1835, by Thomas Maisey, art master at Cheam. This shows the school on its High Street site where Tabor Court now stands.

under a clergyman, George Aldrich, by 1646. He is believed to have lived in the pre-Reformation house now known as Whitehall, in Malden Road, Cheam, described in detail later.

If this is so, he may have taught originally, however, briefly, in Whitehall, traditionally believed to have been the first premises for Cheam School. However, this could have been for a short time only. At the time of the Surrey Hearth Tax Return for 1670 he had two houses, of thirteen and seven hearths respectively, and the smaller may have been Whitehall and the larger the 'School House'. From documentary evidence (see *The Story of Little Woodcote* by Margaret Cunningham, 1989, pp.60-61) the School House was almost certainly West Cheam Manor House, which stood on the site which Cheam Library now occupies and was pulled down at the end of the 18th century. Dr. Daniel Sanxay, whilst headmaster of Cheam School, built a new school on a new site in 1719. This building, which appears on nineteenth century Ordnance Survey maps as the 'Manor House School' stood in Cheam High Street.

One of the best known of Cheam School's headmasters was Doctor William Gilpin (headmaster 1752-1777) immortalised as Doctor Syntax by the writer William Coombe and the caricaturist Thomas Rowlandson. Gilpin had an important influence on the development of art in the late 18th and early 19th centuries, in the movement away from the classical into the romantic or 'picturesque' landscape, an influence which still exists. He was a competent watercolourist and a distinguished art critic.

The Reverend R.S. Tabor became headmaster in 1855, and made the school one of the first preparatory schools. Boys had formerly remained until they were eighteen. In 1934 the school moved to new premises whose address is Headley, near Newbury in Berkshire (Headley itself is in Hampshire). The school is now known as Cheam Hawtreys.

Perhaps best known of the pupils who attended the school at Cheam is Prince Philip, Duke of Edinburgh (Prince Charles, was at the school after its move). Other famous 'old boys' included Henry Addington, Viscount Sidmouth (Prime Minister 1801-1804), Hugh Childers (Chancellor of the Exchequer 1882-1885); Lord Randolph Churchill, father of Sir Winston; and the Marquis of Milford Haven, who was there in 1928-32.

The school in Cheam was pulled down in 1935. Tabor Court, named after two headmasters, father and son, now occupies the site, in the High Street. The early nineteenth century school chapel, now a Roman Catholic church, remains.

12. Whitehall, 1 Malden Road, Cheam, built c.1500; opened to the public through Sutton Heritage Service since 1978.

## Whitehall, Malden Road, Cheam

Built in about 1500, possibly as a yeoman farmer's house, Whitehall was opened to the public in June 1978. It is a very early two-storied, continuous-jettied house, which has been described as one of the loveliest old houses in Surrey.

Extensive alterations began to be made to the house in about the mid-sixteenth century. They include an unusual two-storied porch, a staircase tower, an extra chimney stack (and possibly the conversion of the other one from a timber smoke-bay), and an attic floor. It is conjectured that these extensive additions, giving a dramatic rise in status to the house, may point to a connection at this time with the nearby newly-built Nonsuch Palace; especially since one of the traditional early names for the house is 'Maids of Honour House'.

It is also said to have been once known as 'The Council House', from a belief that Queen Elizabeth I, out hunting from Nonsuch Palace, held an emergency Council meeting there. Whitehall is also said to have gained its present name from being owned at one time by a court official; possibly Edmund Barrett, Sergeant of the Wine Cellar to Charles I. Barrett is commemorated by a tablet in the Lumley Chapel, close by. An attic door in Whitehall bears Charles I's last word on the scaffold: 'Remember'. The name, however, may really derive, as has been recently suggested, from the Cheam sub-manor of Wights.

In the 17th century a further wing was added to the house. The house is timber-framed with an original rye-dough (straw and plaster) infill, much of which remains. Weatherboarding was added at the end of the 18th century to improve draught and weatherproofing.

As already noted, Whitehall is believed to have been connected with the origins of Cheam School. Later it was the home for over two hundred years of the Killick family; until it was sold in 1963 to the then Borough of Sutton and Cheam. The London Borough of Sutton restored it, gaining a Civic Trust Award in 1970. A further restoration was later carried out, and the house is now in the care of Sutton Heritage Service, and run with the support of a charitable organisation, The Friends of Whitehall. A guide to the house is available.

**Worcester Park**

Worcester Park, a locality which lies partly within the north of the Borough, as it did within the old Borough of Sutton and Cheam, is built on part of Nonsuch Great Park, and takes its name from the 4th Earl of Worcester, one-time Keeper of the

13. Central Road, Worcester Park, then Cheam Common Road, at the junction with Longfellow Road, c.1900.

Great Park; the principal house in the Park becoming known during and after his occupancy as Worcester House. The house was on the highest point in the Park, where The Avenue, Royal Avenue and Delta Road meet.

The farms into which the Great Park was divided when Nonsuch was disparked included Worcester Park Farm. In 1865, following the coming of the railway in 1859, the farm and surrounding lands were bought by the Landed Estates Company, who began to erect the modern suburb of Worcester Park. H.G. Wells, who lived there in 1896/7 called it 'Morningside Park' for his novel *Ann Veronica*, published in 1906.

## SUTTON

In the Domesday Book, Sutton appears as Suthtone. The name means South-tun or South-farm (possibly because it was south of a parent settlement, perhaps Mitcham; or possibly because it was the southernmost possession of Chertsey Abbey).

In 1086 the Abbey of St. Peter at Chertsey still held Sutton, as it probably had done for two or perhaps three hundred years. It is curious that two churches were attributed to Sutton by the Domesday Book, but one was probably on an outlying holding at Horley, near the present Gatwick Airport.

There were apparently vineyards in Sutton in the 12th century, since, in 1154, the Prior and Convent of Merton (Merton Priory) are recorded as borrowing forty marks (approximately £26) on the security of their vineyard in Suthtone, Surrey.

Chertsey Abbey held Sutton until 1537, when it was ceded to King Henry VIII in the course of the dissolution of the monasteries. Initially Henry granted it to Sir Nicholas Carew, K.G.; but with his execution and attaint in 1539, it was forfeited, and annexed in 1540 to the Honour of Hampton Court (see under Beddington above). It was returned, along with the other Carew estates, in 1554, to Sir Francis, who kept it until his death. When this occurred, in 1611, and Beddington went to Sir Nicholas Throckmorton (Carew), son of one of Sir Francis's sisters, Anne, Sutton went to Sir Edward Darcy, son of his other sister, Mary. She had married Sir Arthur Darcy, executed for complicity in the 'Pilgrimage of Grace' (a rising in protest against the dissolution of the monasteries).

In 1612 Sir Edward died, and his son, Sir Robert, inherited. The manor was held in 'tail-male'; i.e. only direct male heirs could inherit. The line failing when another Sir Edward, son of Sir Robert, died childless, reversion to the Crown led to a regrant to the Earl of Portland in 1663, in spite of competition from, among others, the Throckmorton-Carews.

In 1669, Thomas, Earl of Portland, sold the manor to Thomas Walcott and Edward Poulter, apparently in trust for a third party, Robert Long, who resold to Sir Richard Mason. Sir Richard Mason left two daughters, one of whom, Dorothy, was married to Sir William Brownlow, Bart. Dorothy Brownlow is the subject of an elaborate memorial in Sutton Parish Church, possibly by William Stanton; now unfortunately hidden behind the church organ.

The sisters, in 1716, sold the manor to an East India Company Captain, Henry Cliffe. It passed then through several more hands. In 1845 it was purchased by Thomas Alcock who helped to build All Saints Church, Benhilton, and rebuild the parish church. He also sold parts of the manor lands for development. By 1912 the manor was held, but without manorial rights, by Norman E. Lamplugh, formerly of Carshalton Place. The title of Lord of the Manor of Sutton is still held, in 1995, by Mr T.R. Lamplugh, President of the Sutton and Cheam Society.

Sutton Manor House stood on a site which is now bounded by the High Street, Benhill Avenue, Nursery Road, and Manor Lane. The house was demolished in 1896. The late Robert Smith, Sutton historian, claimed that some of its chimneys were Tudor, but the sparse photographs that exist seem to show an early-Gothic-revival house; and the manor house of Sutton may have changed its site, perhaps from higher up the High Street hill.

A second Sutton Manor or 'Little Sutton' which existed for a time was once held by Sir Simon de Codyngton, or Cuddington, of the family whose manor was destroyed to make way for Nonsuch.

Sutton in the mid-18th century was an insignificant village centred round the green at the bottom of the hill on which the High Street now stands. Recent archaeological discoveries have now shown, however, that more of medieval and post-medieval Sutton existed on that chalk hill than has previously been supposed.

The growth of Sutton, which, in the 19th century, was to outstrip its neighbours, Cheam, Carshalton and Beddington, stems from the reconstruction of the Brighton Road from London in 1755. This was the main road to Brighton until 1809, when the road through Croydon was opened. The coaches on this road, and the road from Croydon to Epsom via Cheam, crossing it, led to the establishment of coaching inns, notably 'The Cock'. (The Cock Hotel demolished in 1961 was not the original one on this site.) Sutton grew up around these inns, and the toll bars established in the 18th century at the cross-roads. Among the traffic passing through was that to Epsom in its days as a fashionable spa; the Epsom race traffic, later; and the Prince Regent, subsequently George IV, and his friends, on their way to and from Brighton.

A rapid acceleration of Sutton's growth was given by the coming of the railway in 1847; and the commencement of operations by the Sutton and District Water Company in 1863, enabling houses, for the first time, to be built in quantity on the chalk of South Sutton, where, otherwise, deep wells were necessary.

Sutton was at one time famous for the sheep which grazed around it on Banstead Downs: hence the old rhyme which begins 'Sutton for Mutton, Carshalton for Beeves'. It is recorded that, at Ewell Fair in 1831, there were 30,000 Downs sheep for sale.

*The Cock Hotel, Sutton 1740.*

*The Cock Hotel, Sutton 1897.*

14. Two versions of 'The Cock', Sutton's old coaching inn. The earlier one (c.1700 not 1740) was demolished in 1897; the later in 1961.

In 1965, Sutton gave its name to the new local government unit, The London Borough of Sutton, and became the main seat of its administration.

The parish church (St. Nicholas) was rebuilt in 1864. A church appears to have stood on the site since Saxon times. The building demolished in the 1860s probably dated, in part, from at least the end of the 13th century. It was described in 1808 as consisting of a nave and chancel only. Monuments from the old church were transferred to the present one, including the Brownlow memorial mentioned earlier.

## The Gibsons

It is a pity that, unlike Cheam Parish Church, the whole of Sutton's ancient church was destroyed. However, an older building than the present St. Nicholas's Church does survive in the churchyard: the Gibson mausoleum.

This, built in 1777, is the resting place of James Gibson 'Merchant and Citizen of London' and his family. It is also the centre of a mystery, and of a unique annual custom.

The mystery revolves around why the Gibsons are buried here, and the details of their lives, in commerce and, apparently, on at least the fringe of 18th century politics and intrigue. James Gibson was at different times a sailor, a distiller, a wine merchant, a miller, and Master of the Worshipful Company of Ironmongers, one of the Twelve Great City Livery Companies; but he does not seem ever to have lived in Sutton. Nor did the other members of his family who lie there.

The annual observance derives from the will of the last Gibson to be interred in the tomb. Mary Gibson died in 1793, and left

15. The Gibson Mausoleum, in the Parish Churchyard of St. Nicholas, is the centre of a mystery.

money to Sutton Parish Church with the requirement that the tomb should be inspected annually on the 12th of August, when the Rector was to preach a sermon. Originally there was also the distribution of money to the poor.

As far as is known, the public ceremony of opening the tomb had happened every year since 1794, although the money is now absorbed into parochial charities. Many people were attracted to this event, intrigued by the mysteries of the Gibsons, and a book is currently being written on the subject. At the time of writing, however, in 1995, the public nature of the annual inspection has been discontinued.

## Belmont

Belmont is a settlement on the edge of the Downs above Sutton, whose existence followed from the opening of Belmont Railway

Station in 1865. The station was originally called 'California' from a public house nearby called 'The California', a name allegedly given it by the man who built it - a Mr. Joe Gibbons - because he had returned wealthy from the nineteenth century Californian gold rush. It is also alleged that the station's name was changed because freight addressed to 'California' by rail found itself shipped across the Atlantic. It is further alleged that the name Belmont was invented by the stationmaster's wife. Early use of the station was largely the delivery of materials for the building of the old Banstead Hospital, and later for bringing coal for Banstead and Belmont hospitals.

## WALLINGTON

The element 'Wal' in the name means stranger, or Celt, or Briton and, is the same element as the 'Wel' in Welsh, i.e. the name applied to the native population of Britain by the Anglo-Saxon settlers. Wallington or Waleton, then, equals 'WelshTun' and indicates, probably, a Celtic settlement surrounded by the Saxons but coexisting peacefully, as the survival of the name suggests stable continuity.

Wallington was a manor separate from the two Beddingtons at Domesday, and was held by the king. It included two mills (watermills on the Wandle). One virgate (a variable measure of land) was held by Richard de Tonbridge. Henry II granted the manor to Maurice de Creon. It was forfeited for rebellion, but returned to Maurice's son, Peter, in 1215. In 1244 it was granted to one Imbert de Salinis for life 'for a bow of dogwood at Easter', with 'liberty for the king to resume should Normandy and England become one again'. At this time the extent of the manor appears to have been more than fifty acres.

In the 15th and 16th centuries Wallington was in the possession of the Dymokes of Scrivelsby in Lincolnshire. The Dymokes, as holders of Scrivelsby, were hereditary King's Champions, required to throw down the gauntlet at the coronation of a monarch and challenge to personal combat anyone disputing his or her right to the crown. The crest of the arms of the Borough of Beddington and Wallington commemorated this by consisting of a right arm in armour holding a mailed gauntlet.

In 1594 Queen Elizabeth I granted licence to Sir Edward Dymoke to alienate the manor to James Harrington, who in 1596 passed it to Sir Francis Carew.

The Carews already owned property in Wallington. After the execution of Sir Nicholas, his widow, Elizabeth, Lady Carew, wrote a letter to Thomas Cromwell, Lord Privy Seal, asking for relief for herself and her children, and beseeching him to intercede with the King not to take 'that which his grace gave me, which is Bletchingly and Wallyington' and adding 'writtene at Wallyington the xi[th] [11th] daye of March [1539]' (eight days after the death of her husband). Presumably she had already been turned out of Beddington by the King's Commissioners.

Wallington remained with the Carews until 1684, when the then Sir Nicholas sold it. Before 1714 it came to the Bridges family who held it from then on. Curiously, this family has no apparent immediate connection with the Bridges family who acquired the manors of Beddington and Bandon when the Carew estates were sold in 1859.

Wallington was the newest of the old civil parishes which comprise the London Borough of Sutton, since it did not achieve that status until 1867, when its growth, by then outstripping that of Beddington, led to the building of a church (Holy Trinity) and

16. The Town Hall, Woodcote Road, Wallington, built for Beddington & Wallington Borough c.1935.

the hiving off of a new parish, later to have its own Civil Parish Council. The coming of the railway and the building, in 1847, of what later became Wallington Station, had led to this expansion.

The Hamlet of Wallington was then mainly a cluster of small houses: an inn (The Duke's Head) and some larger houses, including Wallington Manor House and the 'Old Manor House' in the Wallington Green area. The inn and some of the smaller houses remain today, as do one or two of the larger, but not the Manor Houses, which went in the early 1930s. What is now central Wallington, was then fields.

The new station, standing some distance from the hamlet, was called Carshalton, since that was the largest nearby place it was built to serve. However, around the station grew up the new Wallington as a dormitory or commuter suburb. Beddington, having no station, lagged behind. By the time the present Carshalton station was opened (in 1868) Wallington was beginning to grow round the old station which then received its present name.

## Beddington Corner

This name can be seen nowadays, publicly displayed, only on a name plate on The Goat public house at Mill Green, Mitcham Junction. The area, like Hackbridge (q.v.), never had a separate official administrative authority. It is where the parish boundaries of Mitcham and Carshalton met at right angles, with the old Beddington parish ending in the corner so produced. The place-naming in this area is very confusing, since this part of Beddington became part of Wallington when the latter parish was formed in 1867. Hackbridge, also with no official boundaries, merges with the southern part of Beddington Corner; and nearby Mitcham Junction Railway Station (over the Borough boundary) gives a postal district name to this part of the London Borough of Sutton.

The small community of Beddington Corner (listed separately in the late 19th and early 20th century directories) was based mainly on the former cluster of Wandle Mills (close to the 'Goat Bridge' which crosses the river at this point) superseded by the present Wandle Trading Estate. There were also market gardens, watercress beds and a lavender and peppermint distillery here earlier this century.

Three public houses served the community, and still exist. The Goat (kid gloves were made hereabouts) and the Skinners' Arms commemorate the leather industry which occupied several of the local mills. A small combined chapel and National School (i.e. Church School) was built on Mill Green in the 19th century and destroyed in the 20th century, having been put to industrial use.

Around the turn of the century there was a Beddington Corner Brass Band. It was here that a branch of the Surrey Iron Railway entered the Borough on its way to the Hackbridge Mills (see under 'Historical Industries in the Borough').

17. Robert's Mill (left) and Aitkins Mill (right) at Beddington Corner, upstream from Goat Road, probably before 1922.

## Hackbridge

Hackbridge is an area with undefined boundaries; most of it within the former Beddington and Wallington Borough, and the Parish of Wallington as created in 1867, but also partly in Carshalton. It takes its name from 'The Hackbridge', the bridge which carries the Carshalton-to-London road over the River Wandle, which at this point formed the boundary between the parish of Carshalton, on the western side, and Beddington and Wallington, on the eastern. The origin of the name, which goes back to the Middle Ages is obscure, but may relate to 'hog' as meaning 'stone' (one medieval version is 'Hogbridge'); therefore, perhaps, a stone packhorse bridge.

The position of the bridge has shifted slightly over the centuries, but here the river was a single stream; whilst back upstream, the Carshalton and Croydon Wandles merged. This, therefore was a convenient place for the bridge. The name eventually came to be applied to the immediate area, merging with Beddington Corner (q.v.) to the north.

In the 18th and 19th centuries the district was one of mills and large riverside estates: the owners of the estates often owning the mills as well. Of some eight houses of substance built in this period, or earlier, standing in grounds ranging in size from an acre to seventy-seven acres, only one, Strawberry Lodge (now church premises) remains. This house had become very dilapidated, and (in 1995) is undergoing restoration of the original house, probably of the Queen Anne period, with the demolition of the 19th century additions.

18. The Hack Bridge, c.1895. The bridge gave its name to the immediate area. This is the cast-iron bridge built in the late 18th century, and replaced in 1912. Note the ford beside the bridge.

# Roundshaw

The newest part of Wallington is Roundshaw, the housing estate built on part of the site of the former Croydon Airport, and occupying roughly the area on which once stood the buildings of the first Croydon Aerodrome (the 'Plough Lane' aerodrome) which was demolished in 1928. The name comes from Roundshaw Park on the edge of the site, itself named from a round 'shaw' or grove of trees, which is still a feature. The estate is a compact one, housing some 8,000 people. It was begun in 1965, with the first tenants moving in during August 1967. Dwellings on the estate are heated from a communal boiler house. It has its own shops, a library, and a community centre; and formerly had its own public house.

A church, opened in 1981, is used by both the Church of England and the Free Churches, which, before it was built, had collaborated in a churchless religious venture known as the 'Roundshaw Experiment'. A cross set up outside the church is made from a four-bladed propeller, or airscrew, obtained through the Croydon Airport Society. The history of the site is commemorated in various ways, including the naming of roads, and the high-rise block of flats (Instone Close) after aircraft, personalities, and firms linked with aviation. One of the schools on the site has been renamed in recent years the Amy Johnson Primary School, after the famous aviator of the 1930s and 40s, the first woman to fly solo to Australia, whose epic flight began at Croydon in May 1930.

The schools on Roundshaw include, since 1975, the famous Wilson's School which moved here from Camberwell in that year. An interesting coincidence is that Sir Alan Cobham, pioneer aviator of Far Eastern and other routes, was at Wilson's School,

19. Roundshaw, on the Croydon Airport site. Note the high chimney of the boiler house, which provides heating for the whole estate.

and that at one time a name under consideration for what became Roundshaw was Cobham Park.

## HISTORICAL INDUSTRIES IN THE BOROUGH

Sutton's connection with sheep farming has been mentioned. As with most similar areas, arable and dairy farming were practised in the district extensively until its character changed with suburban development.

Until this century, the lavender and herb growing industry was extremely prominent in the district. The original centre was Mitcham (Mitcham mint and Mitcham lavender are still used as trade names) and there were extensive fields of lavender and other aromatic and colourful herbs and shrubs, and a number of distilleries in the Borough, especially in the Carshalton, Beddington and Wallington areas.

Cheam was the site of medieval pottery manufacture. In 1923 a kiln base, and many pots, some whole, were found during the excavation of a new road, Parkside, which runs westwards from The Broadway. Of the pottery, some 120 pieces were good enough for museums. Some went to the British Museum, the Victoria and Albert Museum, and Guildford Museum. Some remain in the possession of the present Borough and examples are exhibited in the Heritage Centre and at Whitehall. Cheam pottery was sold in London by its makers, and pieces found in previous excavations in London were already in the Guildhall and London Museums. In 1969 another kiln base was discovered behind 19-23 High Street. A further large amount of Cheam sherds has since been found in an archaeological dig in the grounds of Whitehall, Cheam.

The Wandle industries are a field of study in themselves. The river, in its short distance of about nine miles from its further source (Waddon), to the Thames at Wandsworth, drops 124 feet, or fourteen feet per mile. This is steep enough to have made the river, from early times, an effective source of power by turning water wheels. Of the thirteen mills operating on the Wandle by 1086, seven were in the present Borough. All at this time would have been used to grind corn to flour, but later many diverse trades used the Wandle for power.

The story of the mills is complex, as many mills succeeded each other on the same site, were clustered together, or changed their purpose. Among the important industrial activities were those connected with the cloth industry - fulling; pulping wood to extract dyes; bleaching and printing. The leather industry was especially centred in the Hackbridge area - tanning and parchment manufacture being carried on. The connection with the district of the snuff industry (which may have begun with Ralegh's tobacco) ended with the death in about 1933 of

20. Treading down peppermint for distilling, in Miller's distillery, between Mill Green Road and Wood Street, Beddington Corner, c.1900.

Alexander Lambert, who was born at Lambert's Snuff Mill, Beddington (destroyed by fire in the 19th century), a mill formerly known as 'Sir Walter Ralegh's'.

A recent list complied by milling expert David Jones has found the following trades conducted in the mills on the river Wandle:

| | |
|---|---|
| Corn milling* | Water pumping* |
| Paper making* | Dye making* |
| Cannon boring* | Timber sawing* |
| Felt making* | Gelatine making |
| Tan bark grinding* | Oil seed pressing* |
| Hemp spinning* | Drug preparation* |
| Machine building* | Calico printing |
| Copper working* | Snuff grinding* |

21. Mills above Butter Hill Bridge, 1892. At the end of the 19th century they were owned by Ansell and used for grinding snuff.

Gunpowder making\*    Cloth drying and bleaching\*
Hoop iron rolling    Pencil manufacture\*
Electricty generation\*    Tanning and leather dressing\*

The ones marked with an asterisk were carried on within the Borough boundaries.

One of the major connections of the Borough with transport history was linked to the Wandle industries: the Surrey Iron Railway. This, the first public railway in the world, although horse-drawn and non-passenger carrying, existed from 1803-46, and pre-dated steam railways. The railway ran from Wandsworth to Croydon (later extended as a separately-run line to Merstham) with a branch line across Mitcham Common to Hackbridge. Its purpose was the conveying of minerals and products more speedily than on the bad roads of the time, and it was originally intended to link London with Portsmouth. Some of its track, and stone sleepers, can be seen in a display to be developed in the Heritage Centre garden, in Carshalton.

## Croydon Airport

The other important link with transport history was the presence within the Borough of the first Croydon Aerodrome, cradle of British civil aviation; and of 86 per cent of the later, extended airport: between them, London's chief airport for twenty vital years between the World Wars. Croydon Airport had its genesis in 1915, when a new Royal Flying Corps defence station was formed alongside Plough Lane, Beddington, on New Barn Farm, formerly part of the Carew Estates; and, in 1918, National Aircraft Factory No. 1 was built nearby with its own airfield. The future George VI gained his 'wings' here in 1919 with one of the training squadrons. The airfields were then known as Beddington and Waddon Aerodromes, respectively.

In March 1920 the twin aerodromes were chosen to become the Customs Airport of London (after Hounslow had performed this function for nine months on a temporary basis) and renamed after the nearby town of Croydon.

In 1924, Imperial Airways was formed from the independent British airline operators then using the aerodrome, and in 1928 new buildings were erected along the newly-built Purley Way. Before and after 1928, Croydon was the scene of the start, or finish, of many record-breaking, pioneering and historic flights. Among the highlights are Cobham's return from his five-month African trip in 1926; Lindbergh's visit fresh from the first Atlantic solo flight in 1927; and Amy Johnson's return from Australia in 1930. But, day by day, routine flying continued, building up Britain's air links with the world.

In 1959, after taking part in the air defence of London in the Second World War (Hurricane and Spitfire squadrons took part from here in the Battle of Britain), Croydon was closed, having become too small for major post-war traffic. The Roundshaw housing estate has now grown up on the old aerodrome, but names famous in aviation history have been used for its street names to keep alive the memory of Britain's first major airport.

On May 5th 1980, the Croydon Airport site was reopened for flying for one day when the London Borough of Sutton organised an Airshow and a re-enactment of Amy Johnson's departure on her historic solo flight to Australia which began on that day 50 years earlier.

A second Airshow was organised in 1988 to mark, in Australian Bicentennial year, the 60th anniversary of the first solo flight to Australia by Bert Hinkler, and the airport's many other Australian connections.

22. The new, 1928, Croydon Airport buildings: the Terminal Building, with control tower (middle); the Aerodrome Hotel (front) and hangars (rear).

# FURTHER INFORMATION

## BOOKS

### The Borough as a Whole

Bradley, Ian et al (eds). *All Our Yesterdays: A pictorial record of the London Borough of Sutton over the last Century.* Sutton Leisure Services, 2nd edition, 1991.

Broughton, June (ed). *The Past in Pictures: A further collection of photographs of the London Borough of Sutton over the last century.* Sutton Leisure Services, 2nd edition, 1991.

### Early History

Adkins, Lesley and Roy. *Under the Sludge: Beddington Roman Villa.* Beddington, Carshalton and Wallington Archaeological Society, 1986.

## Historical Industries

Crowe, A.J. *Inns, Taverns and Pubs of the London Borough of Sutton.* Sutton Libraries and Arts Services, 1980.

Festing, Sally. *The Story of Lavender.* Sutton Leisure Services, 2nd revised edition, 1989.

Wandle Group. *The River Wandle: A Guide and Handbook.* London Borough of Sutton Public Libraries, 1974. (Revised edition in preparation).

## BEDDINGTON

Bentham, Thomas. *A History of Beddington.* John Murray, 1923.

Wilks, Michael & Bray, Jennifer (eds). *The Courts of the Manors of Bandon and Beddington 1498-1552*: transcribed and translated by Hedley M. Gowans. Sutton Libraries and Arts Services, 1983

### Carew Manor

Michell, Ronald. *The Carews of Beddington.* Sutton Libraries and Arts Services, 1981.

Phillips, John. *Carew Manor: A Short Guide.* Sutton Leisure Services, 1989.

## CARSHALTON

Jones, A.E. From *Medieval Manor to London Suburb: an obituary of Carshalton.* Author. n.d.

Jones, A.E. *An Illustrated Directory of Old Carshalton*. Author, n.d.

Jones, A.E. *The Story of Carshalton House*. Sutton Libraries and Arts Services, 1980.

## Honeywood

Doug Cluett and Jane Howard. *The Heritage Centre, Honeywood, Carshalton: a brief history and guide*. Sutton Heritage Service, 1994.

## Little Holland House

Dickinson, Frank R. *A Novice Builds his own Ideal House*. Sutton Leisure Services, 1994.

## The Oaks

Cunningham, Margaret. *The Story of the Oaks and Oaks Park*. Sutton Leisure Services, 1993.

## CHEAM

Burgess, Frank. *Cheam Village Past and Present: Comparative views from 1891-1991*. Sutton Leisure Services, 1991.

Burgess, Frank. *Old Cheam: a photographic record and commentary*. Sutton Libraries and Arts Services, 1978.

Marshall, Charles J. *A History of the Old Villages of Cheam and Sutton*. S.R. Publishers, 1971. Originally published in 1936, this book still contains much of value although parts have been superseded by subsequent research.

## Cheam School

Peel, Edward. *Cheam School from 1645*. Thornhill Press, 1974.

## Nonsuch

Dent, John. *The Quest for Nonsuch*. Sutton Leisure Services, 1981. A reprint of the revised 2nd edition, published in 1970.

Lister, Lalage. *Nonsuch: Pearl of the Realm: the story of Henry VIII's fantastic palace*. Sutton Leisure Services, 1992.

## Whitehall

Jackson, Pat. *Whitehall, Cheam: a short guide to the house*. Sutton Leisure Services, 1994.

## SUTTON

Burgess, Frank. *No Small Change: 100 years of Sutton High Street*. Sutton Libraries and Arts Services, 1983.

Burgess, Frank. *Now and Then: More views of Sutton old and new*. Sutton Libraries and Arts Services, 1985.

Burgess, Frank. *Sutton: a pictorial history*. Phillimore, 1993.

Smith, Robert P. *A History of Sutton*. Derek James, 4th edition, 1970.

# WALLINGTON

Whiteing, Eileen. *Anyone for Tennis: Growing up in Wallington between the wars.* Sutton Libraries and Arts Services, 1979.

Whiteing, Eileen. *Some Sunny Day: Reminiscences of a young wife in the Second World War.* Sutton Libraries and Arts Services, 1983.

## Croydon Airport

A multi-volume history of the airport is being published by the Borough's Leisure Services. The first three volumes, jointly written by Douglas Cluett, Joanna Bogle (née Nash) and the late Bob Learmonth are: *The First Croydon Airport, 1915-1928; The Great Days, 1928-1939, and Croydon Airport and the Battle for Britain 1939-40.* A fourth volume is in preparation.

Other books include:

Bamford, Jack. *Croissants at Croydon: The Memoirs of Jack Bamford* (former General Manager at Croydon for Air France), Sutton Libraries and Arts Services, 1986.

Cluett, Douglas. *Croydon Airport: the Australian Connection: Flights and other links.* Sutton Leisure Services, 1988.

Cluett, Douglas. *The First, The Fastest and the Famous: A Cavalcade of Croydon Airport Events and Celebrities.* Sutton Libraries and Arts Services, 1985.

Cooksley, Peter G. *Croydon Airport Flypast: Historic Aircraft Profiles in Colour.* Sutton Libraries and Arts Services, 1984.

Dickson, Charles C. *Croydon Airport Remembered: An Aviation Artist Looks Back*. Sutton Libraries and Arts Services, 1985.

## BUILDINGS OPEN TO THE PUBLIC

The following buildings are opened to the public by Sutton Heritage Service:

**The Heritage Centre, Honeywood,** Honeywood Walk, Carshalton, Surrey (by Carshalton Ponds). 0181-773 4555

**Whitehall,** 1 Malden Road, Cheam. 0181-643 1236.

**Little Holland House,** 40 Beeches Avenue, Carshalton.

**Carew Manor & the Dovecote,** Church Road, Beddington.

**Carshalton House,** Pound Street, Carshalton.

**The Archives and Local Studies Search Room,** Central Library, St Nicholas Way, Sutton, has a large collection of material about the Borough.

**For opening times and other information please ring the Heritage Service on 0181-770 4781/2.**

**The Water Tower** in the grounds of Carshalton House is leased to the Water Tower Trust, whose Friends organisation opens it to the public on Sunday afternoons in the summer season.

**Nonsuch Mansion,** in Nonsuch Park: the kitchens and service areas are opened to the public by the Friends of Nonsuch on the 1st and 3rd Sundays of summer months.